By Craig Bradley

Illustrations by Liz Dale and
Steve McCann

CABOODLE BOOKS LTD

A Catalogue record for this book is available from the
British Library.

ISBN-13: 978-0-9559711-7-4

Typeset in Century by Paul Wilson

Printed in the UK by CPI Cox & Wyman, Reading

The paper and board used in the paperback by Caboodle
Books Ltd are natural recyclable products made from wood
grown in sustainable forests. The manufacturing processes
conform to the environmental regulations of the country of
origin.

Caboodle Books Ltd
Riversdale, 8 Rivock Avenue, Steeton, BD20 6SA
Tel: 01535 656015

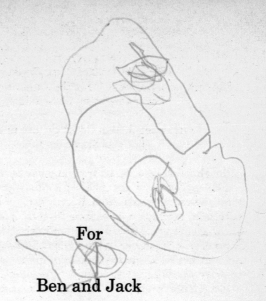

For

Ben and Jack

Contents

The Poet Tree.. 1

I Like To Rhyme It Rhyme It............ 2

Petrolhead... 4

Toast.. 6

Watching Telly With The Sound
    Turned Down 8

Football Star 9

The Sharpest Pencil In The Box...... 10

How To Celebrate A Hat Trick 12

Girl In Goal.. 15

Star Performer....................................... 16

Muddy Windows 18

Sadly, Gladly, Mr Bradley 19

Playing With Words 20

Famous Five 22

Dentist Drill.. 23

Everything Looks Like The Moon ... 24

How Loud Can You Whisper?.......... 26

Really Good Poem.............................. 28

The Fastest Dad 30

Big Letters, Little Letters................ 31

Going Backwards 32

Bottom Of The Page 34

Watching King Kong 35

Bunk Bed Dreams 36

My Window 38

Clouds 39

Bloon 40

If I Won The Lottery 41

My Stuff 42

Teacher, Teacher 44

Mr Jones 46

Poems Are Like Butterflies 47

Laughing Your Head Off 48

Treacle 50

Dawn and Dusk 51

Sometimes My Mind Has A Mind
    Of Its Own 52

Second Hand Shoes 54

Favourite Socks 56

When Did Dinner Ladies Turn Into
    Lunchtime Supervisors? 58

Dad's Hands 60

The Garlic Dalek 61

56 Ways To Look At A Leek............. 62

Five Things Not To Do 66

Cattitude 67

Who Let The Rhymes Out? 68

Chips 72

Waiting For Your Chips
   (In A Chip Shop Queue) 74

Batman's Birthday Party................. 76

Sploot.. 78

Dog On A Diet................................. 80

A Cloud Like Shrek 82

Living Next Door To Spiderman...... 84

Goldfish Don't Bounce..................... 85

A Piece Of The Sky.......................... 86

Bamboozled..................................... 87

Flabbergast 88

Blink... 89

Getting My Haircut 90

Dunking Big Digestives
   In A Tiny China Cup 91

A Good Job 92

Eating Toblerones On Trains 94

Truthpaste 95

The Carpet Under Dad's Chair 96

The Back Of A Spoon 97

Looking Inside Stuff 98

Dead Bird 100

Cold Tea 101

Desk Top 102

Er, Er, Like Y'know 104

Brand New Teacher 106

Corridors 107

Bad Poem 108

I'm Late 110

White Button, Black Shirt 112

That's What It Is 114

The Poet Tree

Every poem you hear
every poem you see
is bright new leaf
on the poet tree.

I Like To Rhyme It, Rhyme It

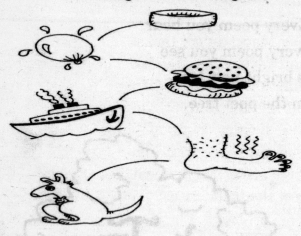

Loop the loop, Hula Hoop
nincompoop, chicken soup
ballyhoo, B&Q
PS2, Scooby Doo.

I like to rhyme it, rhyme it
I like to rhyme it, rhyme it.

Trumpet, crumpet
like it or lump it
waterbomb, Dick and Dom
hubcaps, breadbaps
silly Billy, piccalilli.

I like to rhyme it, rhyme it
I like to rhyme it, rhyme it.

Big Macs, carpet tacks
railway tracks, Halifax
ring-a-ding, ball of string
bling bling, Burger King
bag of chips, Walnut Whips
backflips, lick your lips
high street, on the beat,
feel the heat, cheesy feet.

I like to rhyme it, rhyme it
I like to rhyme it, rhyme it.

Magic wand, garden pond
blue-eyed blonde, James Bond
Kung Fu, U2, kangaroo, outside loo
swimming pool, April fool
big school, stay cool
suitcase, ratrace, fishface, lost in space
bag of slime, it's a crime
loads of rhyme, one more time.

I like to rhyme it, rhyme it
I like to rhyme it, rhyme it.

3

Petrolhead

Suburu, metallic blue
Fiat Panda, one point two
Ford Focus, Ford Fiesta
Vauxhall Vectra, sunroof extra
Honda Accord, Isuzu Trooper
Range Rover, Mini Cooper

    Petrolhead, petrolhead
    amber, green and red, red, red
    Petrolhead, petrolhead
    traffic jam inside my head.

Volkswagon Golf and Polo
Volvo, Clio, Fiat Punto
Shogun Sport, big off-roader
Jaguar, Porsche, Audi, Skoda
Peugeot, BMW
Lexus, Saab and Mazda too.

Petrolhead, petrolhead
amber, green and red, red, red
Petrolhead, petrolhead
traffic jam inside my head.

Satellite navigation
Kwikfit, petrol station
turbo charged, exhaust pipes
alloy wheels, go faster stripes
hatchback, four by four
fuel injection, engine roar
tinted windows, cruise control
automatic, let it roll.

Toast

I like burgers, baps
bacon, scrambled eggs
and mushy peas.
Carrots, grapes, pasta shapes
cauliflower cheese.

I like prawns, shrimps,
mussels, whelks and cockles
by the coast.

But I like toast
I like toast
I like toast the most.

I like crisps, curried fish
peanut butter, Irish stew.
I like Tuna bake, chocolate cake,
soup and pizza too.

I like stir fry, shepherd's pie
spuds and Sunday roast.

But I like toast
I like toast
I like toast the most.

I like pork chop with eggs on top
sprouts and runner beans.
I like chick peas, cheddar cheese
leek and aubergines.

I like Spam, ham, leg of lamb
I don't want to boast.

But I like toast
I like toast
I like toast the most.

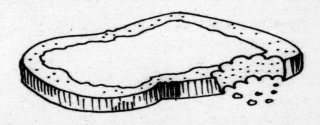

Watching Telly With The Sound Turned Down

Sticking you fingers

in your ears

and walking round the town

is just like watching telly

with the sound turned down.

Football Star

He thinks he is a football star
because his haircut's class.

He thinks he's Wayne Rooney
but he can't shoot or pass.

He thinks that he's a lion
but he's more like an ass.

He walks the walk and talks the talk
but I can see through him like glass.

He's really good on paper
what a shame he's rubbish on grass.

The Sharpest Pencil in The Box

He can play midfield
he can play in attack
he can play in goal
he can play at the back
when he plays in our defence
it's locked tighter than Fort Knox
but he's not the sharpest pencil in the box.

He's brilliant in the air
he's brilliant at free kicks
it's brilliant just to watch him
when everything clicks
he's wicked on the wing
and as cunning as a fox
but he's not the sharpest pencil in the box.

He's a real matchwinner
who's impossible to beat
he's a wizard on the ball
with a magic pair of feet
he looks razor sharp
in his stripy *Nike* socks
but he's not the sharpest pencil in the box.

How To Celebrate A Hat Trick

First Goal

Lick your finger, stick it in the air
wave at the stands and the bench over there
punch the sky, wink at the crowd
sing *We Are The Champions* really, really loud
dance with your mates and the corner flag
smile, be happy, the first one's in the bag.

Second Goal

This is more like it, this is getting serious
you've scored another and everyone's delirious
do the Moonwalk, jump up and down
kiss everybody in the football ground
do the crazy celebration you've rehearsed
the second goal's great, sweeter than the first.

Third Goal

Pull your shirt over your head, run like a plane
you can't believe you've scored again.
look at the camera,
     shout *Wayyyyhhaayyyyy!!!!!*
that'll look wicked on Match Of The Day
listen to the fans, they're screaming for you
it's goal number three, a dream come true.

Girl In Goal

Our team has a girl in goal
we call her Flying Fiona
you don't get that on Sky TV
at Chelsea or Barcelona.

Flying Fi just loves the mud
when it's wet and slippy
but she hates it when our football strip
clashes with her lippy.

Flying Fiona saves headers and shots
and those screaming free kicks that curl,
and every Saturday we all agree
that the man of the match is a GIRL!!!

15

Star Performer

He's a crowd pleaser
goalkeeper teaser
24-carat gold
diamond geezer
cool as a breezer
that's why he's a

Star performer
Star performer

Real barnstormer
real heartwarmer
hotter than a chicken korma
his dad's called Keith
his mum's called Norma

Star performer
Star performer

Man of the match
the one they can't catch
the itch on the pitch
the one they can't scratch
he's a football dream
the best on the team
a dizzying, dribbling
goal machine

Star performer
Star performer

He's a one-man show
a dynamo
just sit back
and let him go, go, go!
he's a real one off
there'll never be another
it's just a shame
he never had a brother.

Muddy Windows

This bus has muddy windows
and even though I try
I can't see a thing
as the world is going by.

I can't see the trees and houses
and I can't see the streets
I can't even see the sweetshop
where I stop and buy my sweets.

I press my nose against the window
and all that I can see
is a picture of my muddy face
staring back at me.

Sadly, Gladly, Mr Bradley

There was a young man called Bradley
who whatever he did, he did badly
he tried his best
but no one was impressed
and that is the truth that is, sadly.

But this persistent young man called Bradley
started writing poetry madly
he wrote day and night
now he's doing alright
and that is the truth that is, gladly.

Playing With Words

I say dinner
You say lunch
I say slap
You say punch.

Playing with words
is just like a game
where two things
can mean the same.

I say kip
You say sleep
I say weirdo
You say creep.

I say settee
You say couch
I say OW!
You say OUCH!

Playing with words
is just like a game
where two things
can mean the same.

I say loser
You say fool
I say wicked
You say cool.

I say mate
You say friend
I say it's over
You say the end.

Famous Five

It's not fair
I've got no hair
spent too long
in the barber's chair.

Whenever I listen
to Britney Spears
I stick my fingers
in my ears.

Football boots
never fit Michael Owen
because his toe nails
keep on growing.

If the Queen
popped in for a bickie,
I've eaten them all
so it'd be a bit tricky.

Elvis is alive
I know it's true
I heard him singing
in the loo.

Dentist Drill

Teeth kill
feel ill
dentist will
use drill.

Very shrill
refill
no thrill
not brill.

Lay still
until
pain nil
chill pill.

Everything Looks Like The Moon

A cherry bun
looks like the moon
The shadow of the sun
looks like the moon
A manhole cover
looks like the moon
Your little brother
looks like the moon.

A blob of grease
looks like the moon
A ten pence piece
looks like the moon
An empty space
looks like the moon
Your best mate's face
looks like the moon.

A big bass drum
  looks like the moon
The nail on your thumb
  looks like the moon
A tennis ball
  looks like the moon
Anything at all
  looks like the moon.

A big balloon
  looks like the moon
A silver spoon
  looks like the moon
Everything
  looks like the moon
Just like the moon
  looks like the moon.

25

How Loud Can You Whisper?

I'm always asking questions
it's what I like to do.
I've got a gazillionbillion questions
and here are just a few.

How loud can you whisper?
How quiet can you shout?
And can you look really serious
if your tongue is hanging out?

How low can you jump?
How slow can you run?
And can you ever finish
before you've begun?

Can you see things without looking?
Can you sit down when you stand?
And can you catch a rainbow
and hold it in your hand?

What do clouds taste like?
How much does your shadow weigh?
And is the day before tomorrow
the day after yesterday?

I'm always asking questions
it's what I like to do.
I've got a gazillionbillion questions
and I bet you've got some too.

Really Good Poem

I like chips
cos they're really good
for snacking.
I like ducks
cos they're really good
for quacking.

I like bubbles
cos they're really good
for blowing.
I like frisbees
cos they're really good
for throwing.

I like bells
cos they're really good
for ringing.
I like songs
cos they're really good
for singing.

I like games
cos they're really good
for playing.
I like jokes
cos they're really good
for saying.

I like beds
cos they're really good
for sleeping.
I like secrets
cos they're really good
for keeping.

I like trees
cos they're really good
for climbing.
I like poems
cos they're really good
for rhyming.

The Fastest Dad

My Dad works for the Council

he's the fastest dad you'll see

he finishes work at five

but he's home by half past three.

BIG LETTERS,
Little Letters

CAPITALS LETTERS
ARE SERIOUS
AND GO AROUND
SHOUTING AT EACH OTHER.

lower case
letters are nice
and quiet
like my little brother.

Going Backwards

Attention! This vehicle is reversing.
Attention! This vehicle is reversing.

It's funny how things change
Attention! This velcro is rehearsing
    the further you walk away from them
Attention! This vulture is revising
    and the further away you go
Attention! This verruca is revolting
    the more they change
Attention! This vinegar is refusing
    and sometimes, even the changes
Attention! This vegetable is remaining
    start changing
Attention! This volcano is revolving
    and it's only when
Attention! This vegetable is remaining
    you start going backwards
Attention! This vinegar is refusing
  that things sound the same

Attention! This verruca is revolting
   and you end up
Attention! This vulture is revising
   back at the very place
Attention! This velcro is rehearsing
   where you started.

Attention! This vehicle is reversing.
Attention! This vehicle is reversing.

Bottom of the Page

I like it down here, it's my favourite place,
no one getting stressed and in my face,
turn the page and I disappear,
but that's OK cos I like it down here.

Watching King Kong

When I saw King Kong
at the pictures he looked
as big as big could be.

But later he looked a lot
smaller when I saw him on DVD.

When I saw King Kong
at the pictures he looked
as angry as angry can be.

He looked like my Dad
when he comes home from work
and I tell him I've eaten his tea.

When I saw King Kong
at the pictures he looked
as real as real could be.

And I'm not surprised
he looked life-like
he was sat in the seat
          next to me.

Bunk Bed Dreams

Bunk Bed, Bunk Bed
That's what I said
Bunk Bed, Bunk Bed
It's gone to my head
Bunk Bed, Bunk Bed
That's what I mean,
Bunk Bed, Bunk Bed
My Bunk Bed Dreams.

The bottom bunk is
    An old ship sunk
    A song unsung
    A ladder's bottom rung.

The top bunk is
    A magic carpet ride
    A plane flying high
    A hammock in the sky.

Bunk Bed, Bunk Bed
That's what I mean
Bunk Bed, Bunk Bed
My Bunk Bed Dreams.

The bottom bunk is
    A fallen down tree
    A raft at sea
    A picnic blanket when it's time for tea.

The top bunk is
    An eagle in flight
    My best mate's kite
    A super duper shiny little star at night.

Bunk Bed, Bunk Bed
That's what I mean
Bunk Bed, Bunk Bed
My Bunk Bed Dreams.

My Window

From here I can see down
our street and the house

with no gate where the big
ginger cat lives.

I can see wheelie bins
with house numbers on

and the terracotta tops
of chimney pots.

I can see tiny pylons spiking
far-away hills and plastic bags,

snagged like clouds
on next-door's tree.

I can see privets, puddles
and other people's front doors,

I can see a lot from my window.
What can you see from yours?

Clouds

Clouds are only cotton wool
    floating on the breeze
waltzing on a sea of blue
    above the dancing trees.

And if clouds are only cotton wool
    a sight sore eyes to please
then the stars are a million candles
    and the moon a piece of cheese.

Bloon

My little brother doesn't bother
much about the rules
of calling things
by their proper names.

He plays games and takes short
cuts through words, a bit like the one
I take through the woods
on the way home from school.

He plucks names out of thin air
like *clod* for cloud and *bid* for bird
but the best one I've ever heard
is the word *bloon*
or balloon to me and you.

Sometimes on windy days you'll see
a loose bloon high in the sky
soaring like a bid above the clods.

If I Won The Lottery

If I won the lottery
   I'd take what I have gottery
      and spend my big jackpottery
         on sports cars and whatnottery
            and move to somewhere hottery.

My Stuff

I've got stuff in the shed
I've got stuff at my Gran's
I've got stuff in my head
I've got stuff in my hands
I've got stuff that no-one understands.
My stuff.

I've got stuff I want to be
I've got stuff I want to say
I've got stuff you can see
I've got stuff locked away
I've got stuff that'll never see the light of day.
My stuff.

I've got stuff in the loft
I've got stuff in the yard
I've got stuff that is soft
I've got stuff that is hard
I've got stuff to put you on your guard.
My stuff.

I've got stuff that is more
I've got stuff that is less
I've got stuff that is raw
I've got stuff that's a mess
I've got stuff I don't know how to express.
My stuff.

I've got stuff at my Gran's
I've got stuff in my hands
I've got stuff that no-one understands.
My stuff.

Teacher, Teacher

History teacher, Mr Joyce
walked with a limp
and had a deep voice.

Science teacher, Mrs McFee
ate dry toast
and drank cold tea.

Maths teacher, Mr Brooking
smoked his pipe
when he thought we weren't looking.

Mrs... Green

Music teacher, Mrs Green
had the longest nails
I've ever seen.

English teacher, Mr Jones
sat in the staff room
and ate buttered scones.

French teacher, Mrs Scott
used to faint in assembly
when it got too hot.

PE teacher, Mr Nash
wore short shorts
and thought he looked flash.

Geography teacher, Miss Row
fancied Mr Nash
and thought we didn't know.

Teacher, teacher, I remember you
and the stuff you used to do.

Mr Jones

Mr Jones laughed a lot
and had a face made for smiling.

He taught English and had cheeks
like happy apples that made him

look like he had just legged
it for the bus or lugged a heavy

wardrobe up two flights of steps.

He spoke in a blokey kind of way
about syllables and full stops

and showed me how to spell
enthusiasm and *unforgettable*.

He made words dance and gave
me a part in all the school plays.

I'll never forget Mr Jones
his *enthusiasm* made my school days

unforgettable.

Poems Are Like Butterflies

Something sparks
and a lightbulb
flickers in your head.

This spark
floats and flutters around
then slowly, slowly
it grows wings.

Thoughts explode
and you start thinking
in bright colours
reds, blues, yellows,

and before you know
you've written yourself
a butterfly
that you've got to let go

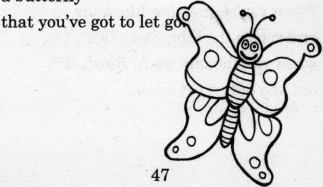

Laughing Your Head Off

When your belly shakes
and your shoulders jiggle
when you know what's coming
is bigger than a giggle.

When you gasp for breath
and your face turns blue
when your legs turn to jelly
and you really need the loo.

When your jaw is aching
and your nose starts to drip
when you make a noise
like a foghorn on a ship.

When you're snorting like a pig
and you're clucking like a hen
when you thought you'd finished
but you only start again.

When your eyes turn to water
and you start to cry
when you're roaring like a lion
and you don't know why.

When you're blaring like a trumpet
and you splutter and you cough
that's what you do
when you're laughing your head off.

Treacle

If you eat too much treacle
    it'll change the way you speakle
because all your teeth will weakle
    and your voice will start to squeakle.

Dawn and Dusk

(Two little poems about big things)

Dawn
is where
the world
stretches and
shakes itself awake
with a big pink yawn.

Dusk
is where
the world
twinkles and
winks to itself
under a blue pyjama sky.

Sometimes My Mind
Has A Mind Of Its Own

Sometimes I say things
I wish I hadn't said
things that I should really keep
locked inside my head
I just say things automatically
like a human answer phone
sometimes my mind has a mind of its own.

I say a lot of things
that people take to heart
I wish I could unsay those things
and make a brand new start
I regret all these silly things
when I'm sitting all alone
sometimes my mind has a mind of its own.

I wish the ground would open up
and make me disappear
I've got to think before I speak
and put my brain in gear
words can be hurtful
you don't need a stick or stone
sometimes my mind has a mind of its own.

Second Hand Shoes

Second hand shoes
Second hand shoes
I'm a bit confused
in my second hand shoes.

These are superhero shoes
    for righting all the wrongs
Shoes for fancy dancing
    and singing all the songs
But who was the man who put his foot
    where now my foot belongs?

Second hand shoes
Second hand shoes
I'm a bit confused
in my second hand shoes.

These are shoes for Saturday night
    and for sucking a sherbet dip
These are shoes for walking in
    and going on a trip
But who was the man who slipped his sole
    where now my sole will slip?

Second hand shoes
Second hand shoes
I'm a bit confused
in my second hand shoes.

These are shoes to sit and think in
    when you're lying in your bed
These are shoes made by a cobbler
    in a shop in Birkenhead
But who was the man trod his toes
    where now my toes will tread?

Second hand shoes
Second hand shoes
I'm singing the blues
I've nothing to lose
I'm a bit confused
in my second hand shoes.

Favourite Socks

My favourite socks
fit just right
they're not too slack
they're not too tight
my favourite socks
are dynamite
they sock it to me
every night
that's why
they're my
favourite socks.

My favourite socks
are not too old
they stop my toes
from going cold
if they had a socks Olympics
they'd win the gold
that's why
there are my
favourite socks.

They're socks to walk a mile in
socks to swim the Nile in
they've got superduper
socktastic styling
when I put them on
I can't stop smiling
that's why
they're my
favourite socks.

My favourite socks
are blue and green
they're the sockiest socks
that I've ever seen
they're a little bit
whhhooaaaggghhh!!!!!
if you know what I mean
that's why
they're my
favourite
I really want to savour it
that's why
they're my
favourite socks.

When Did Dinner Ladies Turn Into Lunchtime Supervisors?

Dinner ladies do the same old job
that they've always done
give you dinner and a drink
and maybe a bun
so we're a bit puzzled
could some one please advise us
When did dinner ladies
turn into lunchtime supervisors?

At dinner time you'll see them waiting
in the dining hall
where everybody charges up to queue
beside the wall
the dinner ladies serve us all
with spoons of different sizes
When did dinner ladies
turn into lunchtime supervisors?

I always eat my dinner
I always clean my plate
I like carrots, pizza, pie and mash
everything is great
but there's one thing that bothers me
as I eat my appetisers
When did dinner ladies
turn into lunchtime supervisors?

I want a real dinner lady
to slice my apple pie
but maybe they're undercover now
and work for the F.B I.
maybe these are robots
wearing cool disguises
When did dinner ladies
turn into lunchtime supervisors?

Come back all you dinner ladies
you know what satisfies us
When did dinner ladies
turn into lunchtime supervisors?

Dad's Hands

My Dad's hands are like mine but stronger
and bigger and longer.

If they could talk they'd have a deep
booming voice and sound like smoky treacle.

They'd tell me about the time he caught a bear
bare-handed, then arm-wrestled a tiger

on the way home. They'd tell me about
painting the backroom and fixing my bike

when the handlebars go wonky
and the horn loses its honk.

If my Dad's hands could talk, I'd listen
and give them the thumbs up.

If your hands could talk what would they say
and would you listen anyway?

The Garlic Dalek

He's a rubbish Dalek

he won't scare you to death

cos you can smell him coming

by the garlic on his breath.

56 Ways To Look At A Leek

It's a frying pan,
a feather duster, or a fan.
It's a tennis racket
or a rocket,
you can keep it in your pocket.
It's a scarecrow's arm
or some shears, it's a big cotton bud
to clean out your ears.

It's a microphone
so you don't have to shout,
it's an umbrella blown inside out.
It's a dart, it's a broomstick,
a mop, a torch, a toothpick.
It's a relay baton that you pass,
it's one massive blade of grass.
It's an ice cream cone, a telephone,
it's a fork, it's a spoon,
it's a brush to sweep the room.
It's a duck's foot, a fly swatter,
it's a wand for Harry Potter.

It's a racing car,
a green guitar,
an exploding joke shop cigar.
It's a sink plunger, it's a key,
or a tiny little tree.
It's a spatula,
a back scratch-ula,
one vampire tooth for Dracula.
It's a telescope,
or a fancy bar of soap.
It's a paddle for a canoe,
it's a shoehorn for a shoe,
it's brush to clean the loo,
it's Ronnie O'Sullivan's snooker cue.

It's a whip, it's a tie,
it's a satellite in the sky.
It's a little lady dancing
in a little grass skirt,
it's a vacuum cleaner
to clean away the dirt.
It's a magnifying glass
for solving crimes,
it's one single human hair
magnified one million times.

It's the torch in the Statue of Liberty's hand,
it's a baton you use to conduct a band,
it's the big hand on the town hall clock,
it's a sticky stick of Blackpool rock.
It's one of Pat Butcher's dangly ear-rings,
a leek is a million different things.

It's a wine glass, a wigwam
and it's the World Cup too.
It looks like Sideshow Bob to me,
what does a leek look like to you?

*Written with the help of the brilliant pupils from
Campsmount College, Doncaster,
Mount St Mary's Catholic School, Leeds and
Aston Comprehensive School, Sheffield.*

Five Things Not To Do

Don't stand on a rake
cos here's how it goes
two holes in your foot
and a broken nose.

Don't walk into a wall
cos here's the score
you'll wish that you
had used the door.

Don't fall out of a window
cos here's the plan
you'll wish you could fly
like Superman.

Don't eat soap
cos here's the deal
the more you eat
the worse you feel.

Don't count your chickens
cos here's the catch
you never know
how many will hatch.

Cattitude

When he's in
    a moggy mood

this cat of mine
    is really rude

a complete lack
    of gratitude

he doesn't drink
    or touch his food

his Whiskers Supermeat
    unchewed

he's a fussy
    feline dude

with bags and bags
    of cattitude.

Who Let The Rhymes Out?

Hairy toes, pick your nose,
see how your garden grows,
red rose, who knows
which way the wind blows,
racing cars, shooting stars,
jam jars, Mars Bars,
uncles, aunts, football chants
Sponge Bob Square Pants.

You'll be honking like a goose
now the rhymes are on the loose.

Who let the rhymes out?
    Who, who, who, who?
Who let the rhymes out?
    Who, who, who, who?

Kick start, poison dart,
heart to heart, custard tart,
Go-cart, work of art,
Homer, Maggie, Lisa and Bart,
traffic cone, Home Alone,
wishbone, saxophone,
buttered scone, the bird has flown,
ringtone, mobile phone.

It's time to get up off your seats
now the rhymes are on the streets.

Who let the rhymes out?
Who, who, who, who?
Who let the rhymes out?
Who, who, who, who?

Milkshake, Jaffa Cake,
chocolate flake, bellyache,
pair of tweezers, summer breezes,
snotty sneezes, Maltesers,
dinosaurs, lion roars,
loud snores, Star Wars,
peanut, papercut,
Big Foot, Pizza Hut,
Sugarplum, sore thumb,
Chewing gum, big fat bum.

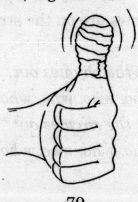

You'll be honking like a goose
now the rhymes are on the loose.

Who let the rhymes out?
Who, who, who, who?
Who let the rhymes out?

Who, who, *who, who?*

Chips

Sometimes
they're too black
sometimes
they're too white
sometimes
they're just too yukky
to bite
and look like they've been
left out all night
but sometimes chips
are just right.

Sometimes
they're too small
sometimes
they're too big
sometimes
you scoff em
and grunt like a pig
your head goes all sweaty
and your trousers
go all tight
but sometimes chips
are just right.

Sometimes
they're too cold
sometimes
they're too hot
sometimes
they look like
they're covered in snot
they're manky and greasy
and have to be binned
cos they make you feel bloated
like a big bag of wind
sometimes chips
are a proper bad sight
but sometimes chips
are just right.

Waiting For Your Chips
(In A Chip Shop Queue)

When you're waiting
for your chips
in a chip shop queue
listen to the frizzle
of the frying fish too
watch the salt
sprinkley dinkle
everywhere
smell the vinegar
biting bitter in the air

read all the postcards
pinned on the wall
advertising builders
and plumbers an' all
feel the money
in your pocket
see the pop piled high
listen to the *PING*
of a microwaved pie

smell the curry sauce
and the slushymushy peas
listen to the chatter
and the *wrapped up please*
there's a list a mile long
of fishywishy things to do
when you're waiting
for your chips

in a chip shop queue.

Batman's Birthday Party

Batman had a birthday bash
  Batbuns, Batcake, Batjelly.
Batman scoffed a load of grub
  and slapped his big Batbelly.

Superman wore his Super shirt
  with a big, red super S on it,
but then he spilt his trifle
  and made a big, red super mess on it.

The Incredible Hulk was in a sulk
  because he ripped his vest.
WonderWoman did a lot of wondering
  but no one was impressed.

Mr Freeze ate all the cheese
    and turned into a block of ice.
The Incredibles popped in for a chat
    and seemed Incredibly nice.

The party lasted all night long,
    everybody had a ball,
except for the Invisible Man,
    no one saw him at all....

Sploot

Is it a planet, lost in space
on the dark side of the moon,
or some detective programme
that's on in the afternoon?

Is it something that you say
when you hammer your thumb,
or a swear word that you mumble
when your bus doesn't come?

Is it something that you dream
when you have a little doze,
or is it what comes out when you
sneeze through your nose?

Is it a weird splooty creature
that lives in Timbuktu?
Is it a little baby owl
that goes too-whit too-whoo?
Is it a waterproof sausage
for a wet day BBQ?

I've have no idea,
I really haven't a clue.
The word is sploot
what it means is up to you.

79

Dog On A Diet

Dog on a diet
dog on a diet
I thought he'd gone quiet
he's a dog on a diet.

He used to bark, growl and howl
    whenever the postman came,
he'd leave his hairs
    all over the chairs
and I would get the blame.
    He used to be into everything
just like a bull at a gate,
    but he's got no time for all that now
he's too busy watching his weight.

He used to wolf down cakes and sweets
    and anything at all,
once he scoffed a pair of shoes
    and ate my old football.
But now he's junked the junk food
    he's stopped with all that lark,
These days he's on the *Slimfast*
    and goes dog-jogging in the park.

He's got a dog aerobics tape
    that's how he spends his days,
pumping iron down the doggy gym
    trying to change his ways.
He's well into all this keep fit stuff
    but I think he's gone too far,
you should be happy just being you
    and be proud of who you are.

A Cloud Like Shrek

Clouds can look like anything
if you let your imagination flow
I've seen clouds like big white horses
galloping through the snow.

I once saw a cloud that looked like a swan
with a really, really long neck
but the very best cloud that I've ever seen
is the cloud that looked like Shrek.

There were two other clouds rolling round
in the sky that looked like Ant and Dec,
but the one in the middle; big, happy and round,
was the one that looked like Shrek.

I couldn't believe it, I stared up at the sky
for so long that I hurt my neck,
but I'll never forget the day that I saw
a cloud that looked like Shrek.

Living Next Door To Spiderman

My neighbour's got a secret
but now I realize
exactly who he really is
behind his web of lies.

I've seen him leap from roof to roof
I've seen him catching flies
I've seen his creepycrawly suit
and his creepycrawly eyes.

I've seen him running really fast
and walking up the wall
and whenever there is danger
he'll be ready for the call.

I've seen him in the comics
and I've seen him on TV
he's the superhero Spiderman
and he lives next door to me.

Goldfish Don't Bounce

Goldfish don't bounce
spiders will not stretch
and Mum's best shoes are not goalposts.

Snakes can't juggle
cows don't mean to stare
and chickens don't like KFC.

Spit is not hair gel
chalk is not food
and boiled egg sandwiches
            are *supposed* to smell like that.

Sprouts are not the brains of small aliens
the remote control does not lose itself
and it never, ever rains on purpose.

Bogies are not collector's items
earwax is not furniture polish
and you cannot sell farts on E-bay.

And goldfish still don't bounce.

A Piece Of The Sky

I've got this jigsaw
of an old man fishing
and the only problem is
there is one piece missing.

There's this old man fishing
and a boat's going by
and the only missing piece
is a piece of the sky.

So this old man's fishing
and he's staring out to sea
and there's a hole in the sky
where the sky should be.

Bamboozled

If you ever feel bamboozled

like you haven't got a cloozled

and you don't know what to doozled

then just take off your shoozled

and have a little snoozled.

You'll soon be good as newzled.

Flabbergast

When a big wagon goes past

and it's going really fast

they make a windy blast

that leaves you feeling flabber

gast.

Blink

Eyelashes are friendlier
  than you think

they kiss each other
  when you blink.

Getting My Haircut

When my hair gets long
    I go to the hairdresser
the scissors snip
    the clippers clip
and my hair gets
    lesser and lesser.

Dunking Big Digestives In A Tiny China Cup

Dunking big digestives
   in a tiny china cup
      is a ridiculous way
         to spend your day
            you might as well give up.

A Good Job

It's a good job
my Mum gets me up
or I'd lay in bed all day.

It's a good job
my mate helps me out
when I don't really know what to say.

It's good job
birds can fly
or how would they get around?

It's a good job
fish can swim
or they'd be flapping all over the ground.

It's a good job
cows make milk
or what would Dad put in his tea?

It's a good job
we've got number 4
or what would we put after 3?

It's a good job
I can learn stuff
or I'd never know how.

It's a good job
I wrote this poem
or you'd be reading nothing

right now.

Eating Toblerones on Trains

If you eat Toblerones on trains

nothing good comes from it

your face goes bumpy

weird and lumpy

and looks like Wallace and Grommit.

Truthpaste

I want to invent some truthpaste
I think it's a good idea
cos all the fibs would vanish
and all the lies would disappear.

If we brushed our teeth with truthpaste
all the children, women and men,
then everyone would tell the truth
and never tell lies again.

The Carpet Under Dad's Chair

The carpet that lives
under Dad's chair
is such a secret place
you hardly know it's there.
It doesn't get a lot
of wear and tear
so it's bright and fluffy
and not threadbare
I think it looks smart
really quite debonair.

It doesn't go out a lot
doesn't go anywhere
like a walk in the park
for a bit of fresh air
it just lives in the dark
and I don't think it's fair
but I can think what I like
it won't really care
it's just the carpet that lives
under Dad's chair.

So there.

The Back Of A Spoon

When I see my face
on the back of a spoon

it goes all weird
like a monster on the moon

or a crazy old guy
from a crazy old cartoon

and everytime I see it
it makes me want to swoon

when I see my face
on the back of a spoon.

Looking Inside Stuff

Inside An Ear

I've got a few facts
about earwax
and there is one
that I have to make clear.
It's absolutely useless
unless you're the inside
                    of an ear.

Inside A Poem

Slapbang
in the middle of a poem
is a place you ought to go

because
that is where the words
and ideas say hello.

Inside A Spider

If you spied inside a spider
you wouldn't believe your eyes
you'd see a bit of spider spit
and a load of chewed up flies.

Inside A Football

I looked inside a football
and I think I must announce
there is nothing there
except some air
that gives the ball its bounce.

Dead Bird

Little dead bird
you used to fly
way up in the sky so high
little dead bird
you used to soar
little dead bird
you'll fly no more.

Little dead bird
you used to sing
and tell the world
when it was spring
little dead bird
you had songs galore
little dead bird
you'll sing no more.

Little dead bird
life was a game
that you would never win
little dead bird
Mum picked you up
and threw you in the bin.

Cold Tea

The sky has many faces
and some of them you'll see
from the deepest of the deepest blue
    to the colour of cold tea.

It's the colour of all the feathers
of a million parrots in a tree
it's the colour of a whisper
    and the colour of cold tea.

It's the colour of the old days
and how things used to be
it's the colour of a memory
    and the colour of cold tea.

It's the colour of your Dad's mad face
when he's lost his front door key
it's the colour of a secret
    and the colour of cold tea.

It's the colour of some pyjamas
that you wore when you were three
it's the colour of a dream
    and the colour of cold tea.

Desk Top

Paperclip
Oh paperclip
you really can't be beat,
you keep my books all tidy
and all my papers neat.

Blu-tac
Oh Blu-tac
you're the best of all
I really like the way you keep
my pictures on the wall.

Ruler
Oh Ruler
I'm glad that you are mine
cos you're the one I turn to
when I want to draw a line.

Pencil
Oh pencil
you get 10 out of 10
if something's wrong, I rub you out
and then I start again.

Notebook
Oh notebook
you know you always win
I like the way you open up
and let my writing in.

Er, Er, Like, Y'know

Sometimes my words
just fade away
and leave me there
with nothing to say
I've got the word
on the tip of my tongue
one minute it's there,
the next it's gone
it's something I can't
put my finger on
but when it happens
I want to shout
when what's inside
just won't come out
instead I just stand there and go
er, er, like, y'know.

It does my head in
I can't explain
but it happens again
and again and again
I only wish I knew the cause
of this thing that puts
my brain on pause
it's like summat in my head
saying *Hang on a mo*
er, er, like, y'know.

The words get stuck
in my head and it won't let go
there's a blockage somewhere
that's stopping the flow
I sound like a broken radio.

Er, er, like, y'know.

Brand New Teacher

Brand new teacher
dark brown hair
sitting in
her teacher's chair

Brand new teacher
looks the part
knows our names
off by heart

Brand new teacher
seems OK
only started
yesterday

Brand new teacher
doesn't fret
hasn't shouted
well, not yet

Brand new teacher
school's a buzz
wonder what
she thinks of us?

Corridors

School corridors have their own laws
dull grey walls and shiny floors
they lead you through a million doors
footsteps deafening like applause

Echoey voices, fluorescent light
always flickering, never bright
turn a corner, left or right
you'll dream about these walls tonight

On and on you walk for miles
scuffling on the lino tiles
past a phone that no-one dials
in corridors where no-one smiles

They'll get you there, get you back
it's easy when you get the knack
right on time, clickety-clack,
like a train upon a track

School corridors have their own laws
dull grey walls and shiny floors
they lead you through a million doors
you'll hear a whisper if you pause

that whispered word is *corridors*

Bad Poem

This is what happens when poems go bad
if you read me now, you'll wish you never had

I'm the kind of poem
that you've never seen before
all my words are ugly
all my rhythms are raw
this poem's gone bad
rotten to the core
if you see me coming
better lock your door

I'm a nasty piece of work
all moody and mean
all my fingernails are dirty
all my teeth are green
my breath is foul
my manners don't exist
I will swat you like fly
with a flick of my wrist

When poems go bad
I'm the baddest round here
I create a certain
atmosphere
I'll say this once
I'll make it clear
to mess about with me
is a bad idea

I'm a nightmare in rhyme I take but never give
I'm a bad, bad poem and I know where you live

I'm Late

I'm late Miss
cos a spaceship Miss
landed down our street
I'm late Sir
cos a whirlwind Sir
whirled me off my feet

I'm late Miss
cos the Vikings Miss
invaded my backyard
I'm late Sir
cos it's snowing Sir
snowing really hard

I'm late Miss
cos my bike Miss
both the tyres were flat
I'm late Sir
cos it's cold Sir
and I couldn't find my hat

I'm late Miss
cos the car Miss
it ran out of fuel
I'm late Sir
cos it's flooding Sir
I had to swim to school

I'm late Miss
cos a pirate Miss
came and stole my pen
I'm late Sir
but don't worry Sir
I won't be late again

White Button, Black Shirt

I'm a big footprint
    in a field of snow
I'm a dandruff speck
    on a red dickybow
I'm a spot
    on a domino
I'm a silver buckle
    on your favourite skirt
I'm a little white button
    on a big black shirt

I'm a white boat
    on a sea of blue
I'm a childproof top
    on a tube of glue
I'm a scrape of chalk
    on a snooker cue
I'm a blue light
    on red alert
I'm a little white button
    on a big black shirt

I'm a feather
    tucked in a cap
I'm a piece of cheese
    in an old mousetrap
I'm the X
    on a pirate's map
I'm a shiny gold coin
    in a pile of dirt
I'm a little white button
    on a big black shirt

That's What It Is

It's a swan's reflection
   in a flatglass pond.
It's moonbeams
   on red roses.
It's the sound of emptiness
   in the back of beyond.
It's raindrops
   on wet noses.
It's the wind whistling
   through broken slates.
It's a bleeding sky
   at sunset.
It's eating fish and chips
   outside with your mates.
It's a prize
   you haven't won yet.
It's away-day trips
   and apple pips.
It's the echo
   in an empty cave.

It's paperclips
    and lipstick lips.
It's making
    a last minute save.
It's the cream in your coffee
    and the sugar in your tea.
It's the very best of you
    and the very best of me.
It's the snazz, it's the jazz
    it's the razzamatazz.
It's the fizz, it's the frizz
    it's the absolute biz.

That's what poetry is.

Craig Bradley is a professional poet, writer and performer who tours the UK sharing his passion and infectious enthusiasm for words.

He performs in schools, libraries, museums, art galleries, hospitals and literary festivals.

He has held many writing residencies in libraries, schools, prisons, youth offending teams, hospitals and literary festivals. In 2003 he was Calderdale Libraries first ever Reader In Residence, and has read his work on radio and TV.

Amongst other things, Craig has been a stand-up comedian, roadie, heavy metal drummer, window cleaner, humbug boiler, nightclub bouncer, Butlins breakfast cook and a gravedigger.